PUNCH LIBRARY OF HUMOUR

Edited by J. A. HAMMERTON

❧ Designed to provide in a series
of volumes, each complete in itself,
the cream of our national humour,
contributed by the masters of
comic draughtsmanship and the
leading wits of the age to "Punch,"
from its beginning in 1841 to the
present day ❧   ❧   ❧   ❧

MR. PUNCH'S GOLF STORIES

THE GOLFER'S DREAM

MR. PUNCH'S GOLF STORIES

TOLD BY HIS MERRY MEN

AND ILLUSTRATED BY

PHIL MAY, GEORGE DU MAURIER, L. RAVEN-HILL, F. H. TOWNSEND, HARRY FURNISS, E. T. REED, BERNARD PARTRIDGE, F. PEGRAM, A. S. BOYD, A. T. SMITH, A. WALLIS MILLS, DAVID WILSON, C. E. BROCK, GUN-NING KING, C. HARRISON, G. L. STAMPA, TOM BROWNE AND OTHERS

WITH 136 ILLUSTRATIONS

PUBLISHED BY ARRANGEMENT WITH

THE PROPRIETORS OF "PUNCH"

🍂 🍂 🍂

THE EDUCATIONAL BOOK CO. LTD.

THE PUNCH LIBRARY OF HUMOUR

Twenty-five volumes, crown 8vo, 192 pages
fully illustrated

THE HUMOUR OF GOLF

THERE are few pastimes that supply their followers with more innocent merriment than is afforded by "the royal and ancient." Certainly no outdoor game can make the neophyte feel more utterly worm-like in his ability, for it is the peculiar quality of golf to appear to be absurdly easy to the onlooker and preposterously difficult to the unpractised player. It may be taken that there is no better way of reducing a man's self-conceit than to place him on the teeing ground for the first time, present him with a driver and invite him to strike a little rubber-cored ball to a distance of 200 yards in a given direction. Consequently we have here most excellent material for fun ; and you may depend upon it MR. PUNCH has not had his eyes long shut to the humours of the links. Despite the royalty and antiquity of golf, it has been thoroughly democratised in modern times, and its popularity, in the wide proportions to which it has attained, is chiefly a matter of recent years. Despite the shortness of the period that is represented by what we may call the vogue of golf—a vogue that is by no means in danger of passing—MR. PUNCH has evidently found the game so rich in fun that his merry knights of the pen and the pencil have contributed to his pages as many pictures as to illustrate very lavishly this volume and a good deal more literary matter than could be used. In the days when croquet was as popular as golf is to-day—the days of Leech and Keene—doubtless a volume could have been drawn from PUNCH devoted entirely to that sport. But it is worthy of note that an examination of these old croquet pictures and jokes for a comparison of them with the contents of the present volume leaves one with the conviction that the humour of the present day is infinitely superior to the humour of the days of Leech and Keene. Admirable draughtsmen though these artists were, both of them, but Leech particularly, were often content to let their masterly drawings appear with the feeblest jokes attached. The standard of humour has been immensely raised of late years, and MR. PUNCH'S GOLF STORIES is no bad evidence of that.

MR. PUNCH'S GOLF STORIES

"GOLFERS AS I 'AVE KNOWN"

(By a Caddie)

GOLFERS I divides in me own mind into three clarses; them as 'its the ball, them as skratches it, and them as neither 'its nor skratches the blooming ball but turns rarnd and wants to 'it or skratch anyone as is small and 'andy. The first clars is very rare, the second is dreadfull plentifull, and the third, thank 'evins, can jeneraly be kep clear of by them as knows the ropes. Sich as meself.

Any himprovement in golfers, as a clars, is doo to the 'uge morril hinfluence of us caddies, 'oom some pretends to look down on. Much can be done, even wif the most 'ardened (and some of them golfers is dreadfull 'ardened), by firmness and hexample. "Show 'em from the fust as you'll stand no nonsense," is allus my words when the yunger caddies gathers ararn me fer hadvice. Me being older than me years, as the sying is, and much looked up to. If, as I often 'ears say, there's less of langwidge and more of golf upon these 'ere links, it's doo in no small part to 'im 'oo pens these lines. 'Oo's 'onnered nime is 'Enery Wilks.

I seldom demmeans meself to speak to the kulprits, for severil reasons which I shall not go into, but I 'ave other meffods. There's sniffing, fer instance. Much can be done by jerdishous sniffing, which can be chinged to soot all cases. Or there's a short, 'ard, dryish larf, but that ain't allus sife. As a blooming rule, I rellies upon me sniff, me smile and me eye. There's few of them as can meet the last when I chuses to turn it on. Not as I objecs very strongly to a little 'onnest cussing; it's hinjustice and false haccusashun as I will not stand.

8

Caddie (visiting). "What kind o' player is he?"
Caddie (engaged). "'Im? He just plays as if it was for pleesure!"

9

Sich are me meffods to them as needs 'em, but don't think, becos at times I'm cold like and 'ard and stern, that I cannot be jentle wif them as call fer jentleness. No blooming errer! 'Enery Wilks is the lad to 'oom old gents in need of keerfull nussing should be hintrusted by their wives and keepers. I'm not allooding now to old tigers 'oos stiple food is red pepper in 'uge quantitties, 'oo turn upon yer like blooming manniacks if yer blows yer nose quite inercent, and 'oo report yer before yer know if you're stand-ing on yer 'ead or yer 'eels. No, I'm not allooding to old gentlemen like them! 'Enery Wilks 'as very little use fer sich unguvverned creetures. In 'is erpinyun they should not be let abrord without a chine. But I am allooding to them 'oos pashuns age 'as tamed, insted of blooming well hincreesed, to jentle 'armless old fellers, 'oo will almost eat out of yer 'and, as the sying is, an sich a one is Mister Perceval Giggington.

Over sixty 'e is, and allus kind and civvil and re.speckfull, but 'e 'as no more haptitood fer golf than a jeerarf. Sometimes I thinks, musing kindly like, as 'ow the old cove 'ud be yunger if

McFoozler (after a steady sequence of misses). "Ah—er—is there a *limit* for these links?"

'e took the gime less seerius. But 'Enery Wilks 'as little to reproche 'imself about ; 'e, at least, 'as done what 'e could to 'elp old Giggs. 'Is wife came down to the Club 'Ouse wif 'im larst Toosday, jest as nice an old lidy as 'e's a gent. She drew me on one side and spoke konfidenshul like, while the old man was fussing and bleeting about 'is clubs. It seems as she'd 'eard of me, and 'eard nuthing but good. Which is only right.

" 'Enery," she ses, " me 'usband 'as set 'is 'art, as you well know, on going rarnd the course in under an 'undred and thirty strokes. It's beginning to tell on 'is 'ealth, the strine and diserpointment, and I want's it stopped. 'E's going rarnd allone wif you now, as the course is clear, and I wants," she ses, " *I wants you to see as 'e does it !*" she ses.

Well, nobody, excep one ignerrant, gellous, preggerdiced skoolmaster, 'as ever dared to call 'Enery Wilks a fool. I took 'er meaning in a moment, and I touched me cap, quiet and konfident like. " Mike yer mind easy, mum," I ses in my korteous way. " It shall be done, this very day, if 'Enery Wilks is spared," I ses.

Policeman. "Where did you get that bag?" *Bill Sykes (indignantly).* "There you are! Nice thing, in a free country, that a man can't have a quiet hundred up without the police interfering!"

She nods and smiles and slips a bob into me 'and, and then old Giggs finishes wurrying abart 'is clubs and we makes a start. The old 'un 'ands 'is card to me to keep, and I speaks to 'im, kind like but firm.

"I'll keep the score, sir," I ses. "Don't yer wurry abart yer strokes at all. What you've got to do is to koncentrite yer mind upon yer gime. For we're a-goin to do it to-day," I ses. 'E 'ears me wif a little sorrerful smile, and I lived up to them remarks. 'E'd arsk me at the end of an 'ole, that 'e'd fairly bitten along, 'ow many 'e'd taken, but I would never tell 'im. I jest kep 'im upon 'is legs wif kindly, jerdishous praise. Even after that 'ole where 'e'd strook me wif 'is ball from the drive, although standing well be'ind 'im, and been in each bunker twice or more, I give 'im a word of 'ope. It was niblick play and 'ope all rarnd the blooming course. And at the end, when I added up 'is card, strike me pink if 'is score weren't an 'undred and twenty-nine! And I sent 'im 'ome to 'is wife, as pleased as any child. There's some, I dessay, as would 'ave made 'is score an 'undred and nineteen or even less, but

14

Jones has recently taken up golf. He is already proficient in one department—the art of addressing the ball,

'Enery Wilks 'as allus known the virtew of modderation.

II.

THERE'S some as takes their golf too seerius fer their strength, like that pore old Mister Gigging-ton, of 'oom I've told yer, and there's some as don't take it seerius enuff. Under this 'eading I places Mister 'Erminius Brellett. 'E's what they call a litterry cove in privit life, and, wifout wishing to be undoolly 'arsh, I must say as I beleeves it of 'im. Strike me pink, if I didn't know as 'e was litterry, I should go away some-times after 'earing 'im talk, and swear a hinfer-mashun of loonacy agin 'im! But Chawley Martin, one of our caddies, 'oo once spoke quite hintermate and friendly like wif a reporter feller, in connecshun wif a biking accerdent caused by Chawley's unforchernate pashun fer trick riding, ses as 'ow all these pore riters is alike. So you and me should only pitty them. As fer 'is golf, exsentrick ain't the word fer it. 'E stands wif both 'is feet quite klose together, springs 'igh into the air wif a tremenjus swing, and strikes the bail

"Keep your head still" is the first rule in golf, and **Binks** means to do so.

afore 'e comes to earth agin. The erstonishing thing is that 'e does strike it abart once in three, and when 'e does it goes like old Gewillikins. It just shows as there ain't no rules abart some peeple's golf. But the sad part is as 'e's quite proud of 'is stile, insted of laberring to kerrect it under my tewishun.

" I'm a mishonnery, a pyoneer of golf, 'Enery," 'e ses to me quite recent. " 'Ow I plays it to-day, the rest of the silly 'ide-bound creetures will play it to-morrow," 'e ses.

" Let's 'ope not, sir," I ses, quite respeckfull and reely meaning the words; fer, if yer think of it, a course full of Mister 'Erminius Brelletts would be an 'iddeous sight. 'E glared at me fer a moment quite dangerous, and then 'e began to larf. What wif 'is livver, at which 'e's allus cussing, and 'is kurious 'arf-irriterble, 'arf-manni-ackal temper, I can tell yer 'e takes some 'andling. But 'Enery Wilks knows 'is 'Erminius Brellett by this time.

" Your one chawnce of fime, you retched child," 'e ses, and I found 'is stile of speaking jest a little gorling, " will rest on the fact that you karried the

18

Short-sighted Old Lady (to little Binks, who is going to the golf-links). " How much will you charge me to mend this umbrella ? "

clubs of 'Erminius Brellett, pyoneer of golf and unerpreshiated riter of himmortal books," 'e ses. Well, yer can't argue wif a man like that. Yer can only yumour 'im by respeckful silence, and be reddy all the time to dodge if 'is manyer turns 'ommersidal all of a sudden.

'E took on Mister Washer the other day, a member 'oom both 'e and I 'ave little liking fer. At least, I can arnser fer meself. Fer 'e's one of your pompus, strutting sort of fellers, 'oo thinks 'e's good at golf, but ain't. I 'eard 'im chalenge Mister Brellett to play a rarnd fer 'arf-a-crown, and a less skilful stoodent of yuman nachure than 'Enery Wilks could 'ave told as they didn't love each other. I 'ad a privit tuppence on the match meself, wif old Washer's caddy, although not very 'opeful. 'Owever, when 'Enery Wilks' money is down, as the sying is, 'e's 'ard to beat.

But things went badly wif us from the start. I could see as 'ow Mister Brellett was wurried abart somethink, and in addition to that 'e was acktaly trying to play a keerful, sientifick gime. Oh, lumme, it was orful, I can tell yer ! We was skarcely touching a ball, and old Washer, as pleesed as

TRIALS OF A NOVICE.—"*Something* must be wrong. That's the third time running I've used this club!"

a turkey-kock but far less hornimental, was playing right above 'isself. Fer a man like meself, 'oo'd staked above 'is means, it was 'art-breaking. We lost five 'oles bang orf, and then Mister Brellett spoke 'arf to me and 'arf to 'isself as we walked to the sixth tee.

" It's all that cussed nime ! " 'e ses. " If I could only think of that, I'd be orlright. A female nime fer a kerrecter in my new book. 'Enery, what's the nime of your yung woman ? " 'e ses, joking like. Well, love ain't much in my line, me ambishuns not letting me 'amper meself wif wimmen, but still a feller 'as to keep 'is 'and in. I won't say as I 'aven't been more run after than most, but some'ow that ain't one of my temptashuns. 'Owever, more to pleese 'er than meself, I lets one of them, jest a school kiddy, walk out wif me at times. She means well, I do believe, but I've allus reckoned as 'ow 'er nime's agin 'er.

" Hervangeline's 'er nime, Mister Brellett," I ses, deprerkating like. " But she can't 'elp it," I ses.

" By Jewpiter ! " 'e 'owls. " Hervangeline's the

! ! ! !

Lily (from Devonshire, on a visit to her Scotch Cousin Margy in St. Andrews, N.B.). "What a strange thing fashion is, Margy! Fancy a game like golf reaching up as far north as this!"

THE HANDY CADDY

Wily Jones sold his big St. Bernard and substituted a tame Caribou, which a friend brought him home from Canada.

IT WAS SO HANDY WHEN GOING OUT GOLFING.

IT MADE SUCH A CAPITAL CADDY.

AND JONES
COULD INDULGE IN EXPLETIVES
WITHOUT BEING A BAD EXAMPLE

IF THE WEATHER SUDDENLY TURNED
OFF COLD HE HAD ONLY TO HELP HIMSELF
TO A TOP COAT;

ALSO IT GAVE
QUITE A PARK-LIKE APPEARANCE
TO JONES' BACK GARDEN

& IF IT RAINED
TO AN UMBRELLA
AND SOU'WESTER.

very nime I've been 'unting for. And now I'll win this match!" 'e ses.

"You'll win it orlright, sir," I ses, ernest like "But, for 'evin's sake, stop playing sientifick! Play the old gime as you're pyoneer on, sir,' I ses.

"I beleeve as 'ow you're right, 'Enery," 'e ses, thoughtful like; and then we come to the tee and watched old Washer drive 'is yusual straight shortish ball. Then Mister Brellett grips 'is club, takes 'is yusual wicked, himmoril stance, springs 'igh into the air wif an 'arf-styfled yell, and, by Gewillikins, drives sich a ball as the pro. 'isself might 'ave been proud on! It knocked the kowardly 'art out of old Washer, did that tremenjus drive; and 'e's a man as only plays 'is best when 'e's winning easy. They 'ad a narsty lead, but we stuck to 'em like wax, 'itting a turriffick ball once out of three, or even oftener, and we won at last quite 'andsomely by three and two.

I remember as I bought bull's-eyes fer Hervangeline wif that 'ere tuppence, becos in a meshure, as you may say, she'd 'ad an 'and in the winning of it. 'Owever, wif a jenerosity unyusual in wimmen,

27

she hinsisted on sharing 'em wif 'Enery Wilks, 'oos skilful leedership 'ad reely won the match.

III.

TAKING it all in all, 'Enery Wilks 'as very little use for wimmen. Excep, of course, as playthings and rellaxashuns after toil. As sich I regards Hervangerline, of 'oom I've told yer. That is, when 'er mood is dosile. At sich times, when she is not trying to be yumourous or utherwise acting the goat, the child can listen, wif doo respekt, whilst 'im she loves so well unbends 'isself. It is 'er privviledge to see 'Enery Wilks remove 'is stern cold marsk. Yuss, I tollerates Hervangerline, but I 'ave little use fer uther wimmen.

Speaking quite frenkly, I can find little to kommend in the hexeckertive of these 'ere links, but there is one of their resent hinnervashuns in pertickler that fills me wif cold rage. This is the rule permitting lidy members to play on the course, excep' on Satterday and Sunday.

Lord knows as 'ow the men is bad enuff to deal wif. 'Eadstrong, vain, irriterble and pig-'eaded

"THE BOGEY COMPETITION"

they mostly is, but oh! strike me pink and purple, if they ain't fair angels, wings and all, kompared to those dredfull, onreasoningable wimmen! Onreasoningable is the one word as I can use to deskribe them. And that don't do 'em justise.

Wif a man, to some eggstent, you do know where you are. You do know from eggsperiense 'ow fur you may go wif 'im, before 'e katches you a clump on the side of the 'ead. But wif wimmen no eggsperiense will 'elp yer. Becos there ain't no rules abart them.

Lord knows as 'ow I started out wif the idear of pleesing 'em. I ses to Hervangerline, the evening I 'eard abart it, "We're going to 'ave lidies on the course, kid," I ses. "Your 'Enery will 'ave to smarten 'isself up a bit fer their dear sakes," I ses. Womanlike she begun to snif.

"You take care, 'Enery Wilks," she ses worningly. "You take care of them desining 'ussies. There's many of 'em as will be after you, I knows it well. Fer some wimmen," she ses, sort of sarkastic, "some wimmen will go after any-think in trarsers," she ses. Well, I wears nickers

Little Albert (always thirsting for knowledge). "Uncle, do they pronounce that ricochaying or ricochetting?"

1.

" Carry your clubs, guvnor, for sixpence ! "
" No, thanks, I don't require a caddie."

2.

" Carry yer clubs for fourpence, boss ! "
" Go away, boy, I'll carry 'em myself."

32

3

Carry 'em for thrippence, mister "
(no response).

4.

A smash !

5.

(*After the smash*). " I say, captain, I'll carry *your* clubs for nothin', *jist for the fun of the thing !*"

meself as a general rule, but I knowed what she meant. And, though of course I 'id it from her, pertending to be kontemptewous, I found 'er words quite pleesing. I thort to meself, komplasent like, as 'ow some of these lidy members might show a prefferrence fer that one of our caddies as is pollished and korteous and older

34

MR. PUNCH'S PATENT CADDIE CAR

than 'is years. But, apparriently, both I and Hervangerline was rong—iddeously rong.

Fer it's no good konseeling from meself, at anyrate, as 'ow I 'aven't been a komplete success so fur wif our lidy members. Why sich should be the case I cannot tell, but there it is. There's a preggerdise agin me as is kep' alive by the ontiring, revengfull tungs of Miss Trigsie Kornish and Missis Jossephus 'Askins. And this is 'ow that preggerdise begun.

Golf is now being played on the Norman Coast

They come along one morning and say as 'ow they're going to play a rarnd, and they'll share a caddy between them. And to my ondying greef they picked on 'Enery Wilks. Not as there was anythink surprising in their doing that. In their place I'd 'ave picked on 'im meself. And I'm bound in justise to say as there was nothing in *their* appeerance to set me agin them. Missis 'Askins is very yung and plessant-looking, although she *is* married, and Miss Kornish is darkish and carries 'erself wif a sort of swing. No, their looks was rite enuff; it was only their dredfull 'abit of cheating as made the trubble.

They started as frendly as love-birds, but by the second 'ole the fur was beginning to stand

Golf is being played very much in Egypt

up stiff upon their backs. It was their orful onguvernabul keenness as did it. On the third green Missis 'Askins asks Miss Kornish 'ow many she's played, and she tells 'er, nine, quite brisk life. Now both Misses 'Askins and meself *knew* quite well as 'ow Miss Kornish 'ad played ten; indeed, I could see as ow Misses 'Askins thort it were eleven. They rangles a bit abart it, growing gradewally more 'eated, and then Misses 'Askins erpeals to me, and I gives it in 'er favour, trying very 'ard to rap it up plessant like. Miss Kornish glares at me like a cat 'oom you've mannidged to 'it wif a brick whilst it's taking a stroll quite inercent and leshurely; but she doesn't say much and we goes on.

Two 'oles later it all 'appens agin, only this time it's Missis 'Askins 'oo 'as kondescended to

37

redooce 'er score. They rages rarnd upon the green, and then Miss Kornish erpeals to me, and truth kompels me to erward the 'ole to 'er. This time it's Missis 'Askins 'oo glarnces at me as though she'd like to cut orf my yung life. But 'Enery Wilks can stand a lot of that.

So we goes on agin, wif the air growing 'eavier like, and three 'oles later they both erpeals to me, fer both is cheating. It was an 'ard posishun fer a yung feller as is only wishfull to pleese. 'Owever, I desided to give pore old Truth another chawnce; although misdoubtfull. So I ses to them quite respeckfull like, as 'ow both their scores is inakkerite and should I keep them both in fuchure?

Oh Lumme, I'd like to forgit what 'appened then! All in a moment those two young wimmen grew frendly agin to each other and konsentrited all their rage and spite on 'Enery Wilks. They fell upon me wif their tungs, and I felt as though I was being 'it wif barbed wire and nettels. They called me "impudent little boy," me the chosin 'ero of the yunger caddies, and I could only garsp and trimble. Their crewel thretts brought

A NEW DISEASE—THE GOLF TWIST

The above caddie (in the course of his third round with Colonel Foozle, who always takes out a collection of two dozen clubs, if only for the look of the thing) begins to doubt if he, the caddie, really belongs to the idle classes, as stated in the papers.

tears even to my proud eyes, and I almost beleeve as 'ow I grovvellel before them. It 'urts me to remember it.

When at last they 'ad tired themselves out, they finished their rarnd as though they 'ad never 'ad an unkind thort towards each other, and I slunk be'ind them, dased and silent, like a puppy 'oos been kicked.

"HOW'S THAT, UMPIRE?"

Golf Player. "Now then, what are you grinning at, boy? Don't you know where the ball is?"

Caddie. "Yus, sir, I know, sir. Please, sir, that there dun cow 've swallered it!"

SCENE—*Country Police Court*

Magistrate. " My boy, do you fully realise the nature of an oath ? "

Boy. " Well, I oughter, considerin' the times I've caddied for yer ! "

*Miggs and Griggs, who have got away for a week-end holiday,
have strayed on to the golf links, and have been watching
the colonel, who has been bunkered for the last ten minutes—
and the language ! !*

Miggs. " What's he doing ? "
Griggs. " *I* dunno. Think he's trying to kill something."

43

And that's—that's what comes of edmitting wimmen to a golf corse !

IV.

YUMIN nachure is a kurius thing. I dunno whether this thort 'as okkurred to other peeple, but I sees the truth of it more clearly every day. You may studdy a man fer weeks and think as 'ow you know 'im inside out, and then, when you try to make some use of 'is pecooliarities, they ain't working that day, or else some little hannoying trifle spiles your well lade skeems. Sich was the sad case of Mister Hoctavius Glenwistle and my friend Chawley Martin.

Mister Glenwistle is an oldish jentleman now, but in 'is day 'e 'as been a famus eggsplorer. Jeograffy never being my strong point, I dunno egsackly where 'e went eggsploring, or why 'e did it. Chawley Martin, 'oo's jenerally 'is caddie, is my hinformant, and some days 'e will 'ave it that Mister Glenwistle would once 'ave reached the Pole if 'is boots 'adn't guv out, and at other times 'e hinsists that it was Africer that 'e visited. I dunno, meself ; per'aps the old jentleman 'as been

Mr. Mothdriver, the famous, yet absent-minded, golf-naturalist, invariably carries a butterfly-net in his golf-bag—for he agrees with Mr. Horace Hutchinson that some of the best entomological specimens can be captured in the course of playing the royal and ancient game.

to both them regins in 'is time. But any'ow all is agreed that once 'e lived for nearly three weeks upon an oldish poodle dawg—which is an orfull thort.

Sich an eggspeerience must leeve its mark upon any man, 'owever strong. It 'as left its mark upon Mister Hoctavius Glenwistle. Every blade of 'air 'as vannished from 'is skalp, and 'is face is a sort of dark brick colour wif light eyebrows. 'E still suffers from sunstroke, and Chawley Martin 'as to carry a large red umbereller round the links to pertect 'is 'ead.

I dunno whether it's the sunstroke, or whether it's 'is ondying remorce for that pore faithfull poodle, but Mister Glenwistle suffers terrible from absent-mindedness. 'E 'as been known to swing up 'is great, red umbereller upon the tee and try to drive wif that, and Chawley Martin allus 'as to watch 'im keerfull to see what 'e'll be up to next. 'E 'ates to be disturbed when in one of 'is mooning fits, and is apt to swear terrible in some forrin' langwidge, which Chawley thinks is Eskimo ; but still 'e's a jentleman all over, is Mister Hoctavius Glenwistle. 'Is tips is 'andsome, and it don't give 'im no pleshure to repport an 'armless lad.

46

Brer Rabbit. " I suppose you haven't seen such a thing as a golf-ball about anywhere, have you ? "

One Sunday lately 'e came down wif a frend for an 'ole day's golf. Chawley Martin, as yusual, was 'is caddie, and I ondertook the manidgement of the frend. All went well in the morning, excep' that Mister Glenwistle fell into a sort of dream upon the seventh green and 'ad to be rarsed by Chawley. It may 'ave been Eskimo that 'e spoke to the boy when 'e'd touched 'im jently on the arm, but it sounded wuss—much wuss.

'Owever, we comes back at one to the club-'ouse, red umbereller and all, like *Robbinson Crewso*, and they goes into lunch. Whilst they're still laying into the grub like winking, I and Chawley Martin, 'aving eaten our own frugil meal, sit down near the 'club-'ouse and begin to polish up their clubs. We fell a-talking about the great science of golf, getting quite 'eated in a little while, and at last Chawley, to illerstrate 'is own mistakin theery, gets upon 'is 'ind legs. 'E takes Mister Glenwistle's best driver from 'is bag and shows me what 'e calls "a full swing, wif every ounce of weight and rist and mussel crammed into it."

I was afeard 'ow it would be. The length of the

48

First Enthusiast. "I say, will you play another round with me on Thursday?"

Second Enthusiast. "Well, I'm booked to be married on that day—*but it can be postponed!*"

club mastered 'im. 'E 'it the onoffending turf a crewel blow, and there was a narsty crack. 'E sits down beside me wif a garsp, and we looks at Mister Glenwistle's pet driver wif the 'ead 'arf off.

"What's to be done, 'Enery?" 'e ses, after a sort of sickly pawse.

Fer my part I'd been thinking 'ard, me brain being better than most.

"There's three courses open to you, Chawley, me lad," I ses quietly. "You can do a guy at once, and not come back—that's one; or you can tell Mister G. as you've been fooling wif 'is clubs —that's another," I ses, and waited fer 'is risponse.

"Let's 'ear the third," he ses gloomily.

"Deceat is aborrent to my nachure," I ses. "But you're made diferent, Chawley. You could make use of 'is absentmindedness and let 'im think as 'e broke it 'isself. 'Old it out to 'im wif a sort of winning smile, when 'e comes, and say as 'ow you're afrade it will 'ave to be mended after all. It's a fair sportin' chawnce," I ses.

"'Enery, you're a fair marvel!" 'e ses, after

50

THE GOLF STREAM.—Flows along the eastern coast of Scotland during the summer and autumn. (Vide *Report of British Association—Section V*).

pondering fer a minute. "I'll try it on," he ses. And so we left it.

I didn't see the meeting between Mister Glenwistle and 'is well-meaning caddie, becos my klient sent me to get him a ball, but when I came back I seed as 'ow Chawley was sniffing slightly, and 'is large outstanding ears was reddened. 'Is manner was coldish like to me, but when the two 'ad drivin, I asked 'im what 'ad 'appened.

"'E just boxed me ears," Chawley ses, "and told me as 'ow 'e'd repport me if I lied to 'im agen," 'e ses.

Fer once I was reely taken aback.

"I can't make it out, Chawley," I ses. "Where was 'is yusual absentmindedness? It just shows as 'ow you can't depend on nuthing in this world! Did you do as I told you, winning smile and all?" I asks 'im.

"Yuss, I did," 'e ses, snappish like. "But it seems as 'ow 'is interfeering frend 'appened to look out of the club-'ouse when I was showing you that swing, and seed it all. Anuther time you can keep your winning smiles and your fat-'eaded hadvice to yourself, 'Enery Wilks!" 'e ses.

52

REAL ENJOYMENT.—*Non-Golfer (middle-aged, rather stout, who would like to play, and has been recommended it as healthy and amusing).* "Well, I cannot see where the excitement comes in in this game!" *Caddie.* "Eh, mon, there's more swearing used over golf than any other game! D'ye no ca' that excitement?"

I didn't answer 'im, remembering 'ow 'is 'uge progecting ears was tingling, but I ses to meself ' So much, 'Enery Wilks, for yumin gratitood ! "

V.

A LITTLE success at golf, as I've notised jenerally makes a man wish for more. Like the appertite of a young girl for chocerlates. I dunno if you remember that nice old Mister Giggington, of 'oom I told you. Under my skillfull gidance and with the ade of a little inercent 'anky-panky 'e kontrived to wander rarnd these 'ere links in an 'undred and twenty-nine. Well, ever since that serprising triemph, 'e 'as been 'ungering for fresh feelds to konker, as you might say.

" I want to meet someone, 'Enery, as I can beat," 'e kep' saying, quite truckewlent like. " I don't pretend as 'ow I'm brillyent, but on my day I do fancy that there's wuss."

" You keep on practising steddy, sir," was my invariable words, " and one of these days we shall see you winning cups and medils."

As nice and kind an old jentleman as ever smashed a club is Mister Giggington, but I allus

A RULING PASSION.—*Mr. Meenister MacGlucky (of the Free Kirk, after having given way more than usual to an expression "a wee thing strong"—despairingly).* "Oh! Aye! Ah, w-e-el! I'll hae ta gie 't up!" *Mr. Elder MacNab.* "Wha-at, man, gie up gowf?" *Mr. Meenister MacGlucky.* "Nae, nae! Gie up the meenistry!"

'ave to 'andle 'im like eggs to prevent 'im losing 'art. I didn't think as 'ow even 'Enery Wilks would be able to grattify 'is 'armless ambishun, but the uther day I saw my chawnce.

It was a Toosday morning, and the course was quite disserted, excep' for Mister G., 'oo was waiting to start a practice rarnd wiv 'is pashunt teecher. Which is me. And then a new member come along 'oo was wishfull for a game, and dirrectly I set eyes on 'im, somethink, hinstink, I suppose, seemed to tell me that 'ere was the man for 'oom I 'ad been waiting.

'E was French, and I shall not attempt to rite 'is name, the 'ang of which I never reely kawt. 'E was a small, darkish, jornty man, and 'is garmints was a little briter and more cheerfull-looking than you see in England. 'E wore, among uther things, a deer-storker 'at wiv a fevver stuck in it. But 'is manners was reely bewtifull. It was quite a site to see 'im click 'is 'eels togevver, and bow to my himployer, and in a minute they 'ad fixed their match. I 'ad 'inted to Mister G. that 'e must hinsist on 'aving a stroke an 'ole, and that was 'ow they settled it. I never lerned what the

A POSER.—" Farmers always grumbling ?   Well, sup-
posin' your pigs were down wi' th' fever, an' your sheep
had got th' influenza, if your crops were drownded in
eighteen inches o' water, an' your rent were overdue—
what would you do ? "

"I ?   I'd give it up and start a golf club ! "

Frenchman's 'andicap was, but if the Champyon 'isself 'ad offered to take strokes from 'im 'e would 'ave closed gladly wiv the offer. And yet there was reelly nuthing erfensive about the little man.

I could see as 'ow pore old Mister G. was trimbling wiv a sort of serpressed egsitement, and I wispered to 'im that 'e must play steddy and use the niblick whenever possibul. The niblick, from long practice in the bunkers, is 'is club.

Me frend, Chawley Martin, was the French-man's caddie, and 'e took ercasion to remmark to me that we seemed in for somethink warmish. I checked the boy wiv one of my glawnces, and then we waited while 'is hemployer took the 'onner. That jentleman danced up to the tee, waving rarnd 'is head the longest and the bendiest driver that I 'ave ever seen, and 'e didn't trubble to address the ball at all. 'E just sprung at it and 'it it wiv all 'is might, and somethink fairly wistled past Chawley's 'ead as 'e stood a little be'ind the tee box. The Frenchman 'ad sliced at rite angels, and for anythink I know 'is ball is still in the air. Certingly, we never saw it agin.

That slite misforchune appeered to egsite and

INGRATITUDE

Brown. " Why doesn't Walker stop to speak ? Thought he knew you ! "

Smith. " Used to ; but I introduced him to the girl he married. Neither of them recognises me now ! "

"Putting" on the "links"   The "tee" and the "caddie"

dimmoralise Chawley's himployer, 'oo may 'ave been quite a brillyent player on 'is day, and I may say at once that 'e never reelly found 'is game. On the uther 'and it seemed to put new life and vigger into Mister G. Our erponent was appariently trying 'ard to do each 'ole in a brillyent one, but we was quite content to win them in a steddy nine.

We 'ad our misforchunes, of course. 'Is deerest frend wouldn't 'ardly say as 'ow Mister G.'s game is a long one, and each bunker seems to 'ave a sort of magnettick attrackshun for 'is ball, but whilst the Frenchman's brassey remained un-broken we knew that there was allus a chawnce for the 'ole. For 'arf the rarnd it stood the crewel strane and then it didn't break. It jest seemed to

GOLF

(*As " Put " by D. Crambo Junior.*)

A showy manner of
handling the " clubs "

A full drive

A beautiful " iron " shot

The " spoon "

The " cleek "

" Holed out "

A MORNING PERFORMANCE

sort of dissolve into small peaces. But we was two
up by then and our tails was 'igh in air.

As for the Frenchman, 'is meffods at times was
reelly serprising. After that first drive Chawley
lade 'isself down flat when 'is hemployer drove,
but even in that posishun it didn't seem 'ardly
safe. That long, thin, bendy driver sent the ball
to all 'ites and all angels, but never once in a
strate line. After a wile 'e diskarded it, and guv a
fair, 'onnest trial to every club in 'is bag in turn.
I should never 'ave been serprised to see 'im drive
desperit like wiv 'is putter, but even then Chawley
wouldn't 'ave dared say nuthink. 'E was quite a
plessant, jentlemanly little man, but it didn't do to

62

FORE !

"Now, sir, be judge yourself, whether I in any just term
am affin'd to love the Moor."

[*Othello*, Act 1., Sc. 1.

63

argue wiv 'im. 'E begun to scream and stamp at once, and Chawley saw pretty soon that it was best and safest to let 'im play 'is own game.

It was on the fiftienth green that the great match was ended. Mister Giggington's pluck and stamminer 'ad been amasing for 'is age, but the strane and the joyfuil egsitement was beginning to tell on 'im. The Frenchman tried to bring off a thirty-yard putt to save the 'ole, and failed by some forty yards. But 'e took 'is defeet like a nero. They shook 'ands on the green and 'e said that it warmed 'is 'art to reflect on the glory that 'is frendly foe 'ad won. I beleeve as 'ow there was tears in the old jentleman's eyes. 'E turned to me and I quite thort 'e was going to grasp my 'and, but instead of that 'e put a bob into it which was pretty near as good.

'E 'll never make a golfer, but 'Enery Wilks will allus be pleesed and proud to gide 'im rarnd the course.

VI.

'ONNESTY is the best pollicy, and, 'Evin knows, 'Enery Wilks 'as allus tried 'is levil best to live up to them golden words. But I reckon there is

"Denmark is the latest of the Continental nations to receive golf.' —*The Tatler.*

But golf must have flourished at Denmark in Hamlet's time, judging by the above reproduction of a very ancient mural decoration which has just come to light.

See also quotation *Hamlet*, Act II, Scene 2:—" . . . drives; in rage, strikes wide!"

certain excepshuns to the cast-iron 'onnesty of all of us, and every yumin being 'as 'is little weakness. Mine is golf balls.

Tips is well enuff in their way, and I 'ave nuthing at all to say agin them, but the present of a good ball is far more pleesing to the 'art of 'Enery Wilks. Praps it's becos of 'is allmost inkonquerabul pride which shrinks at times from taking munney from them 'oom 'e feels to be 'is equils or hinfeeriors; or praps it grattifies 'is artistick nachure to be given the himplements of that great sience which 'e onderstands so well. Any'ow golf balls is my temptashun, and one which once or twice in the course of my 'onnerabul kareer I 'ave allowed meself to yeeld to.

Some golfers will ercashunally 'and you tuppence or an 'arf-used ball, wif a jenial word of thanks for your attenshuns which is worth more to a proud nachure than the gift itself. And there's uthers 'oo never think of doing nuthink of the sort. Among *them* is Mister Schwabstein, 'oo is not French or Scotch, as you might think from 'is name, but German, wiv praps a touch of Jentile.

ENCOURAGEMENT.—*Professional Golfer (in answer to anxious question).* "Weel, no, sir, at your time o' life, ye can never hope to become a *player*; but if ye practise hard for three years, ye may be able to tell good play from bad when ye see it!"

'E's a man what catches the eye on the links, it being 'is constant and hannoying 'abbit to were a peaked yotting cap, large specks, and a white silk coat which was once a good deal whiter. An egsellent sort of person, I dessay, in the 'ome sircle, but 'ardly what you'd call a brillyent success upon the links. They say as 'ow 'e 'as more munney than 'e ritely knows what to do wiv, but I fancy 'e's made it by never giving any of it away 'Owever, 'Enery Wilks 'as done 'is best to put that rite.

Let me diskribe to you a rarnd which 'e played the uther day wiv Mister 'Erminius Brellett, our litterry member, 'oo allus seems to go out of 'is way to play wiv kurious people. I 'ave taken Mister Schwabstein in charge before, but never 'ave I seen 'is pecooliarities so noticeabul as on that day.

'E took the 'onner, and for about three minutes 'e addressed the ball wiv 'is 'uge, thick, ugly driver, which 'as always rarsed my perfessional hindignashun. 'E swung at last, quite slow like, but wiv all 'is great weight and strength piled into it. I shall never know egsackly what 'e did, becos the

Bertie (to caddie, searching for lost ball). "What are you looking there for? Why, I must have driven it fifty yards further!"

Diplomatic Caddie "But sometimes they hit a stone, sir, and bounce back a terrible distance!"

69

tees was dry, and for the moment I was 'arf blinded by the dust. But there was a thud and a krackling snap, and two things was flying through the thick, dusty air. Them two missils was the ball and the 'ead of the driver, and they fell togevver thirty yards from the tee. 'E said something which I couldn't catch and didn't want to, and walked rarnd in a slow sircle, smiling to 'isself. 'E's a man 'oo allus smiles. It often seems to me that it is 'is misforchune.

Then Mister Brellett took one of 'is yusual springing drives, which 'appened to come off, and 'e won that fust 'ole on 'is head. Mister Schwab-stein kontrived to redooce 'is brassey to fragmints at the second 'ole ; and after that he took out 'is niblick, and nuthing wouldn't perswade 'im to put it back. 'E drove wiv that niblick, and 'e played 'is many shots through the green wiv it. And the way that thick strong niblick eat into the turf was enuff to brake the 'art of 'Enery Wilks. We moved slowly forward, leaving be'ind us a line of crewel deep kassims, which nuthink wouldn't fill up. And 'is stile of bunker play was equilly distruck-tive.

Old Hand. "Ah, I heard you'd joined.   Been round the links yet?"

New Hand.   "Oh, yes.   Went yesterday."

Old Hand.   "Whot did you go round in?"

New Hand.   "Oh, my ordinary clothes!"

'Is noshun of getting out was to distroy the wall of the bunker wiv reppeated blows, and then to force 'is ball throo the rewings. I wouldn't 'ave belleeved that meer wood and iron could 'ave done the work that that one German niblick did wivout turning an 'air.

'E only smiled 'is slow smile when Mister Brellett or meself venchured a remmonstrance, and 'e would never pick up 'is ball. 'E persevered wiv each 'ole until at last 'e 'ad pushed the ball into the tin, and then 'e would turn and pat my 'ead wiv 'is large 'and. After the fust time I jenerally dodged, and once 'e turned and patted Mister Brellett's 'ead by accerdent. Like most litterry jents, the latter is rather touchy, and there was neerly trouble; but some'ow, thanks to Mister Schwabstein's apparent onconshusness of offense, it was erverted.

At the thirteenth 'ole Mister Brellett was five up. Mister Schwabstein put down a new ball, wiv a sort of groan, and pulled it wiv 'is niblick right rarnd into the rough. For a long two minnutes we 'unted 'igh and low, but nowhere could we find that ball. If I'd seen it I would 'ave handed it

GOLFING AMENITIES. (*Overheard on a course within 100 miles of Edinburgh*).—*Hopeless Duffer (who continually asks his caddy the same question, with much grumbling at the non-success of his clubs).* "And what shall I take now?" *His Unfortunate Partner (whose match has been lost and game spoilt, at last breaking out)* "What'll ye tak noo! The best thing ye can tak is—he fower fifteen for Edinburgh!"

73

over at once, sich being my boundin dooty. But I never did see it. There was jest one little place in that rough where some'ow it didn't seem worth while looking. We 'ad to erbandon it at last; and Mister Schwabstein lost the 'ole and the match.

Later in the day I wandered down on a sort of ferlorn 'ope to that bit of rough, and kuriously enuff I walked bang on to that ball. There was severil courses open to me. I might 'ave 'anded it over to the orthorities, or I might 'ave kep' it as a memmentoe of Mister Schwabstein's unfaling jenerosity and kortesy. But 'Enery Wilks didn't see 'is way to doing either of them two things. 'E jest disposed of that fine new ball to the very best hadvantage.

———

THE PEDANTRY OF SPORT.—*First Golf Maniac.* I played a round with Captain Bulger the other day.

Second G. M. When did you get to know him?

First G. M. Oh, about the end of the Gutty Ball period.

Cheerful Beginner (who has just smashed the Colonel's favourite driver). "Oh, *now* I see why you have to carry so many clubs!"

TEE, TEE, ONLY TEE!

(Song of the Golf Enthusiast.   After Thomas Moore)

Air—"*Thee, thee, only thee.*"

THE dawn of morn, the daylight's sinking,
Shall find me on the Links, and thinking,
Of Tee, Tee, only Tee!

When rivals meet upon the ground,
    The Putting-green's a realm enchanted,
Nay, in Society's giddy round
    My soul, (like Tooting's thralls) is haunted
      By Tee, Tee, only Tee !

For that at early morn I waken,
And swiftly bolt my eggs and bacon,
    For Tee, Tee, only Tee!
I'm game to start all in the dark,
    To the Links hurrying—resting never.
The Caddie yawns, but, like a lark,
    I halt not, heed not, hastening ever
      To Tee, Tee, only Tee !

Of chilly fog I am no funker,
I'll brave the very biggest bunker,
    For Tee, Tee, only Tee !
A spell that nought on earth can break
    Holds me.   Golf's charms can ne'er be *spoken ;*
But late I'll sleep, and early wake,
    Of loyalty be this my token,
      To Tee, Tee, only Tee !

———

GOLF caddies are now very much in the public
eye.   The education of some of them is certainly
not all that it should be.   " Here's an honour for
us ! " cried one of them excitedly the other day,
as he pointed to a paragraph in the paper headed,
" King Alfonso visits Cadiz."

THE SCIENCE OF GOLF

[A certain make of field-glasses is advertised just now as "suitable for golf-players, enabling them before striking to select a favourable spot for the descent of their ball." There can be little doubt that this brilliant hint will be further developed, with some such results as those outlined in the following anticipation.]

As I told Jones when he met me at the clubhouse, it was a year or more since I had last played, so the chances were that I should be a bit below form. Besides, I was told that the standard of play had been so raised——

"Raised? I should just think it has!" said Jones. "Why, a year ago they played mere skittles—not what you could properly call golf. Got your clubs? Come along then. Queer old-fashioned things they are, too! And you're never going out without your theodolite?

" Well," I said with considerable surprise, "the fact is, I haven't got one. What do you use it for?"

" Taking levels, of course. And—bless me, you've no inflater, or glasses—not even a wind-gauge! Shall I borrow some for you?—Oh, just

78

A LAST RESORT.—*Miss Armstrong (who has foozled the ball six times with various clubs).* " And which of the sticks am I to use now ?" *Weary Caddie.* "Gie it a bit knock wi' the bag !"

as you like, but you won't be able to put up much of a game without them."

"Does your caddie take all those things?" I asked, pointing to the curious assortment of machinery which Jones had put together.

"My caddies do," he corrected. "No one takes less than three nowadays. Good; there's only one couple on the first tee, so we shall get away in half an hour or so."

"I should hope so!" I remarked. "Do you mean that it will be half an hour before those men have played two shots?"

"There or thereabouts. Simkins is a fast player—wonderful head for algebra that man has —so it may be a shade less. Come and watch him; then you'll see what golf is!"

And indeed I watched him with much interest. First he surveyed the country with great care through a field-glass. Then he squinted along a theodolite at a distant pole. Next he used a strange instrument which was, Jones told me, a wind-gauge, and tapped thoughtfully at a pocket-barometer. After that he produced paper and pencil, and was immersed apparently in difficult

Caddie (in stage whisper to Biffin, who is frightfully nervous). "Don't you get nervous, sir It's all right. I've told every one of 'em you can't play!"

sums. Finally, he summoned one of his caddies, who carried a metal cylinder. A golf ball was connected to this by a piece of india-rubber tubing, and a slight hissing noise was heard.

"Putting in the hydrogen," explained Jones. "Everything depends upon getting the right amount. New idea? Not very; even a year ago you must have seen pneumatic golf balls—filled with compressed air? Well, this is only an obvious improvement. There, he's going to drive now."

And this he did, using a club unlike anything I had seen before. Then he surveyed the putting-green—about half a mile away—through his glasses, and remarked that it was a fairish shot, the ball being within three inches of the hole. His companion, who went through the same lengthy preliminaries, was less fortunate. In a tone of considerable disgust he announced that he had over-driven the hole by four hundred yards.

"Too much hydrogen," murmured Jones, "or else he got his formulæ muddled. Well, we can start now. Shall I lead the way?"

Fitzfoozle (a beginner, who is "teaching" a lady on the men's links, and loses a club). "Pardon me, sir. Have you seen a lady's club anywhere?"

Admiral Peppercorn (very irate at being delayed, wishes ladies would play on their own course). "No, sir; but there's a goose club at the 'Pig and Whistle,' I believe. Try that!"

I begged him to do so. He in turn surveyed the country, consulted instruments, did elaborate sums, inflated his ball.

"Now," he said, at length settling into his stance, "now I'll show you."

And then he missed the ball clean.

. . . Of course he ought not to have used such language, and yet it was a sort of relief to find *something* about the game which was entirely unchanged.

———

ROYAL AND ANCIENT RECORDS.—The *Glasgow Evening Times* displayed the following headings on the occasion of His Majesty's visit to North Berwick :—

VISIT TO THE GOLF COURSE.

A DRIVE THROUGH THE TOWN.

This, of course, constitutes a new record, the old one standing at about 330 yards.

———

THE GOLFER'S FRIEND AFTER LONG DRIVES —The Tea-Caddy.

———

GOLF MOTTO.—The "Hole" hog or none.

84

Golfer, whose ball has lodged under stone, has had several unsuccessful shots, and finally, with a tremendous stroke, smashed his club.

Old Man. "You put me in moind of my old jackass."
Golfer. "What d'you mean, you idiot?"
Old Man. "Yer 've got more strength than knowledge!"

THE MOAN OF THE MAIDEN

(After Tennyson)

GOLF! Golf! Golf!
  By the side of the sounding sea;
And I would that my ears had never
  Heard aught of the "links" and the "tee."

Oh, well for the man of my heart,
  That he bets on the "holes" and the play;
Oh, well for the "caddie" that carries
  The "clubs," and earns his pay.

He puts his red coat on,
  And he roams on the sandy hill;
But oh! for the touch of that golfer's hand,
  That the "niblick" wields with a will.

Golf! Golf! Golf!
  Where the "bunkers" vex by the sea;
But the days of Tennis and Croquet
  Will never come back to me!

VIRGIL ON GOLF.—"Miscueruntque herbas et non innoxia verba." *Georgics*, 3, 283.

TO CORRESPONDENTS. — "An Inexperienced Golfer" writes to inquire whether what he has heard about "the Tee Duty" will in any way affect the "caddies."

WILLING TO COMPENSATE.—*Mrs. Lightfoot.* "Oh, wait a minute, Mr. Sharp—don't drive yet. My husband is still on the green." *Mr. Sharp.* "Never mind. I'll risk it. For if I *do* bowl him over, why, I'm ready to replace him any time!"

CAPABLE CADDIES

RUMOUR has it that a movement is on foot amongst a certain section of the golfing public to ensure that for the future all caddies on English links shall be compelled to furnish satisfactory proof that they are physically and morally quali-fied for the porterage and cleaning of clubs, and acquainted with the more rudimentary principles of the game. To this end, it is reported, an entrance examination paper is in course of pre-paration, in which individuals aspiring to official recognition as caddies will be required to obtain a percentage of at least eighty marks. The follow-ing questions are said to have been already drafted:—

1. Write your name, legibly if possible, in the top right-hand corner of the sheet.

> (Do not trouble to insert your nickname, as it is a matter of indifference to the examiners whether you are locally known as "Tiger," "Ginger," or "Bill Bailey.")

2. State your age. If this is less than six, or

STIMIED.—*Golfer.* "Fore!" *Tinker.* "What?" *Golfer.*
'Get out of the way!" *Tinker.* "What for?" *Golfer.* "I
might hit you." *Tinker.* "Thee'd best *not*, young man!"

more than seventy-five years, you may omit the remaining questions and retire at once from the examination.

3. Are you married or single? Give reasons for your answer.

4. Illustrate the finer points of distinction between

    (*a*) a niblick and a gutty;

    (*b*) a bye and a bulger.

5. Are you a Protectionist or a Total Abstainer?

6. Rewrite the following passage, correcting anything that may strike you as an error or an incongruity :—" In an 18-hole match, X., a scratch player with a handicap of 20, stood dormy 12 at the 17th hole, but while half-way through the final green was unfortunate enough to get badly bunkered behind the tee-box. Being required to play 'two more' to his opponent Y., who had laid himself dead in 6, he only played one of them, thus holing out in 5, and securing a victory by the narrow margin of 4 up and 7 to play."

7. Given that the regulation charge for a round is a shilling, would you consider yourself justified in attempting to exact an extra half-crown for

Licensed Caddy. "Carry your clubs, sir?" *Jones (who has chartered a small boy at a cheap rate).* "No I've got a caddy." *Licensed Caddy.* "Carry your caddy, sir?"

club-cleaning from a player in spectacles, with a handicap of 27 and a wistful expression? (Candidates are advised to say "No" to this question.)

———

"As She is Spoke."—(*In the train from Nice.*) *Enthusiastic Golfer* (*to friend, as train stops at Golfe-Juan*): "Oh, here we are! This must be the place. '*Golfe*,' golf. '*Juan*,' *jeu*, play, you know. Yes, this is evidently the station for the links!"

———

The Natural Crest of every Golf Club. —The lynx.

———

Five-o'clock "Tees."—Suburban golf.

THE RULING PASSION.—*Laden and perspiring stranger.* "Could you kindly tell me how far it is to the station?" *Sportsome Native.* "About a full drive, two brassies and a putt."

THE GOLF WIDOWS

(After E. B. Browning)

Do you hear the widows weeping, O my brothers,
    Wedded but a few brief years ?
They are writing home complaining to their mothers,
    And their ink's suffused with tears.
The young lads are playing in the meadows,
    The young babes are sleeping in the nest ;
The young men are flirting in the shadows,
    The young maids are helping them, with zest.
But the young golf widows, O my brothers,
    Are weeping bitterly,
They are weeping in the playtime of the others,
    While you 're swiping from the tee.

Do you ask their grazing widows in their sorrow
    Why their tears are falling so ?
" Oh —yesterday—to-day again—to-morrow—
    To the links you ALWAYS go !
Your golf ' shop,'" they say, "is very dreary,
    You speak of nothing else from week to week ;
A really patient wife will grow a-weary
    Of talk about a concentrated cleek."
Yes, the young golf widows, O my brothers,
    Do you ask them why they weep ?
They are longing to be back beside their mothers,
    While you 're playing in a sweep.

" ——HE WOULD HAVE SAID "

A beautiful stroke missed! A favourite club broken! No words to bring relief!

American Friend (in the background, after a long pause). 'Wa'al, Brown, I guess that's the most profane silence I've ever listened to!'

And well may the widows weep before you
　　When your nightly round is done;
They care nothing for a stymie, or the glory
　　Gained by holing out in one.
" How long," they say, " how long in careless fashion,
　　Will you stand, to drive the Dyke, upon our hearts,
Trample down with nailèd heel our early passion,
　　Turning homeward only when the light departs?
You can hear our lamentations many a mile hence,
　　Can you hearken without shame,
When our mourning curseth deeper in the silence
　　Than a strong man off his game?"

"A BEAUTIFUL DRIVE."

SUBTLE.—"Aren't you a little off your game this morning, Mr. Smythe?" "Oh, I'm not playing this morning, Miss Bertha. Only just amusing myself."

SHOULD MARRIED MEN BE ALLOWED TO PLAY GOLF?

(Extract from a Golfer's Diary)

July 21.—Played Robinson, who would never win a match if it wasn't for his wife. Think that I shall start a links for bachelors only. (Mem.— Suggest to the committee that no married man is allowed to play golf in the mornings or afternoons.)

Hole I. I played perfectly, holing beautiful long putt. Robinson hopeless. One up.

Hole II. R. bunkered. Entirely his own fault. Two up.

Hole III. Holed my approach, allowing for both wind and slope of green ; really a grand shot. Caught sight of Mrs. R. as I walked to the next tee. Three up.

Hole IV. Thought that I might have to speak to Mrs. R. at any minute. Missed my drive in consequence. Disgusting ! Two up.

Hole V. R. seemed to be looking for his wife instead of attending to what I was saying. My

"SHE WAS NOT A GOLFER"

Husband. "What on earth has happened to my driver?"

Wife. "Oh, I couldn't find the hammer, so I used that thing. It wasn't much use, though."

drive lay on a buttercup, and who the deuce can be expected to play off buttercups? One up.

Hole VI. Stymied R. quite perfectly. He pretended to think that we were not playing stymies. We were. Two up.

Hole VII. Saw Mrs. R. looking aimlessly out to sea. These loafing ladies are enough to put any man off his game. Why can't they do something? One up.

Hole VIII. R. may say what he likes, but he waved to his wife. I was also annoyed by his stockings, which I should think Mrs. R. knitted. The sort of useless thing she would do. All square.

Hole IX. Got well away from Mrs. R., and though my caddy coughed as I was approaching I laid my ball dead. Beautiful shot. One up at the turn.

Hole X. Had the hole in my pocket when R. laid his approach dead. Ridiculous luck. All square.

Hole XI. Just as I was driving I saw Mrs. R. still looking at the sea. I complained, but R. took no notice. At any rate she cost me the hole. One down.

OUR VILLAGE
The Golf-Club in full swing.

She. "Why, Mr. Smith, you don't mean to say you have taken up golf?"

Smith (age 78). "Yes. I found I was getting a bit too old for lawn tennis!"

Hole XII. Vardon couldn't have played better than I did, and even R. had to say "Good shot!" twice. All square.

Hole XIII. As I was putting I had a feeling in my back that Mrs. R. had arrived at last. Missed my putt and only halved the hole.

Hole XIV. Couldn't see Mrs. R. anywhere. Wondered where on earth she had got to, or whether she was drowned. Of course I lost the hole. One down.

ERRATIC

Pedestrian (*anxious for his safety*). "Now, which way are you going to hit the ball?"

Worried Beginner. "Only wish to goodness I knew myself!"

Hole XV. A little dispute, as R. claimed that his ball—which was under a wheelbarrow—was on ground under repair. Absolutely foolish, and I told him so. All square.

Hole XVI. Made a perfect drive, approach and putt. Looked everywhere for Mrs. R. and couldn't see her. One up.

Hole XVII. Completely put off by wondering when I should see Mrs. R. Most unfair. Told my caddy I should report him to the committee. All square.

Hole XVIII. Saw Mrs. R. on a hill half a mile away. Got on my nerves. R. said, " Halloa, there's my wife ! I thought she wasn't coming out this morning." Lost the hole and the match, and told the secretary that R.'s handicap ought to be reduced.

SWEET SIMPLICITY

Diffident Man (who does not know to how much of an ingénue he is talking). "Have you been out long, Miss Grace?"

Miss Grace (consulting her wrist-strap). "Oh, about three-quarters of an hour. You see we were asked to come punctually."

LINES ON THE LINKS

HARD by the biggest hazard on the course,
Beneath the shelter of a clump of gorse,
Secure from shots from off the heel or toe,
I watch the golfers as they come and go.

I see the fat financier, whose "dunch"
Suggests too copious draughts of "fizz" at lunch :
While the lean usher, primed with ginger beer,
Surmounts the yawning bunker and lies clear.

I see a member of the House of Peers
Within an ace of bursting into tears,
When, after six stout niblick shots, his ball
Lies worse than if he had not struck at all.

But some in silent agony endure
Misfortunes no "recovery" can cure,
While others, even men who stand at plus,
Loudly ejaculate the frequent cuss.

An aged Anglo-Indian oft I see
Who waggles endlessly upon the tee,
Causing impatience of the fiercest kind
To speedy couples pressing from behind.

Familiar also is the red-haired Pat
Who plays in rain or shine without a hat,
And who, whenever things are out of joint,
"Sockets" his iron shots to cover point.

Before ten thirty, also after five,
The links with lady players are alive,
At other seasons, by the rules in force,
Restricted to their own inferior course.

Foreigner (who has "pulled" badly, and hit his partner in a tender spot), "Mille pardons, monsieur! My clob—he deceived me!"

One matron, patient in her way as Job,
I've seen who nine times running missed the globe;
But then her daughter, limber maid, can smite
Close on two hundred yards the bounding Kite.

*   *   *   *   *

Dusk falls upon the bracken, bents and whins;
The careful greenkeeper removes the pins,
To-morrow being Sunday, and the sward
Is freed from gutty and from rubber-cored.

Homeward unchecked by cries of " Fore ! " I stroll,
Revolving many problems in my soul,
And marvelling at the mania which bids
Sexagenarians caracole like kids;

Which causes grave and reverend signiors
To talk for hours of nothing but their scores,
And worse, when baffled by a little ball,
On the infernal deities to call;

Which brightens overworked officials' lives;
Which bores to tears their much-enduring wives;
Which fosters the consumption of white port,
And many other drinks, both long and short.

Who then, in face of functions so diverse,
Will call thee, golf, a blessing or a curse ?
Or choose between the Premier's predilection
And Rosebery's deliberate rejection ?

Not mine to judge : I merely watch and note
Thy votaries as they grieve or as they gloat,
Uncertain whether envy or amaze
Or pity most is prompted by the craze.

Tommy. " I say, do you know who's winning ? "
Ethel. " I think uncle must be—I heard him offer to carry auntie's clubs."

THE HOLE CONCERN

SCENE—*Any golf-club where an alteration of the course is in prospect.* TIME—*Any time, from dawn to dusk.* CHARACTERS—*Any number of* Members, *plus (on this occasion) an* Inoffensive Stranger.

First Member (*catching sight of* Inoffensive Stranger). Look here, Nobbs, you're an impartial judge, we'll have your opinion. What I say is this. If you take the present 4th hole and make it the 13th, putting the tee back ten yards behind the 12th, and carry the lower green fifteen yards to the right, and play the 2nd, 5th and 16th holes in reverse order, keeping clear of the ditch outside the 4th green, you'll bring——

Second Member. Oh, that's rubbish. Anybody with a grain of sense would see that you'd utterly ruin the course that way. My plan is to take the first three, the 11th, and the 14th—you understand, Nobbs?—(*slowly and emphatically*) the first three, the 11th, and the 14th.

Inoffensive Stranger. Yes?

A TOWN MOUSE

Jones. "Well, my little man, what are *you* thinking about?"

London Boy (who has never been out of Whitechapel before). "I'm thinkin' it's time yer mother put yer into *trousers!*"

Second M. (*quickly*).   And leave 'em as they are. Leave 'em just exactly as they are.   Then you do away with the next, make the 3rd into the 7th, and——

I. S. (*horribly confused*).   But——

Third M.   Yes, I know—you're thinking of the crossing from the 14th.   And you're perfectly right.   Simply fatal, that would be ; too dangerous altogether.   What we really want is a 2nd hole, and my plan would make a splendid one—really sporting, and giving these gentlemen who fancy their play a bit to do.

Second M.   Don't know about *that.*   Tried that patent 2nd hole of yours this morning out of curiosity.   Holed it with my third, and might have done it in two, with a bit of luck.

Third M. (*whistles expressively*).   Oh, *come* ! Splendid player you are, and all that—handicap's fifteen, isn't it ?—but there aren't *many* of us who would stand here and say calmly that we'd done a hole of 420 yards in three !   *Really*, you know——

Second M.   420 yards ?   130, you mean.

Third M. (*defiantly*).   420, if an inch.

A MARTYR TO APPEARANCES

Young Lady. "I say, caddie, what *does* Mr. McFadjock do with all these clubs?"

Caddie (wofully preparing to follow his tyrant). "He makes me carry them!"

Second M. But look here, you told me yourself only yesterday——

Third M. (*slightly taken aback*). Oh, ah, yes. I understand now. I *did* think, at one time, of making the 2nd a short hole. But this is quite a different idea. Miles better, in fact. It flashed across me quite suddenly at dinner-time last night. Sort of inspiration—kind of thing you can't account for—but there it *is*, you see.

Fourth M. Well, what you fellows can argue about like this beats me altogether. There's only one *possible* way of improving the course, and I showed you the plan of it last week. It won't be adopted—not likely. So good, and simple, and inexpensive that the committee won't look at it. Couldn't expect anything else. Anyhow (*with an air of unappreciated heroism*)—I've done *my* best for the club !

(*Sighs heavily, and picks up a newspaper.*)

Fifth M. (*brutally*). Oh, *we* know all about that blessed plan of yours. Now, I'm open to conviction. Mind you, I don't condemn anybody else's scheme. All that *I* say is, that if a man doesn't see that my plan is the best, he's a dunder-headed

LINK(S)ED SWEETNESS

The Real Caddie (audibly). "This club is going to ruin—allowing all these ladies to join!"

Miss Sharp. "They evidently can't get gentlemen!"

jackass, and that's all about it. What do *you* think, Mr. Nobbs?

I. S. (*rather nervously*). Well, really—I hardly know—perhaps——

First M. (*compassionately*). Ah, it's those whin below the 17th that are bothering *you*. But if you exchange the 8th and the 10th——

Second M. (*abruptly*). Rot!

[*The battle continues. The* Inoffensive Stranger *stealthily withdraws.* (*Curtain.*)

Sanguine Golfer. " Is that on the ' carpet,' caddie ? "
Caddie (as the ball swerves into cottage window). " Yus, sir ; front parlour, sir ! "

THE OLD TYPE OF LINK MAN.

Supper time.

THE NEW TYPE OF LINK MAN.

Tee time.

"A THREE-CARD LAY"

LONG ago in Sweet September,
Oh! the day I well remember,
I was playing on the Links against the winsomest
of maids;
In a "cup" my ball was lying,
And the "divots" round were flying,
And with eyes-a-dance she said to me, "Your
iron's the King of Spades!"

Now a foe, on such occasion,
Of the feminine persuasion,
Fair and twenty to the game a sort of subtlety
imparts;
And I felt its potent glamour,
And I answered with a stammer
Shy and nervous, "It was rash of me to play the
Queen of Hearts!"

Any further explanation
Of my inward admiration
Very likely had exposed me to the deadliest of
snubs!
But a snigger from behind me
Just in time came to remind me
Of the presence of my caddie—and I blessed the
Knave of Clubs!

GLORIOUS UNCERTAINTY

SCENE—*At the Golf Club.*

She. "Good-bye, Major. What's the programme for to-morrow?"

The Major. "Oh, either skating or punting, according to the weather."

GOLF AND GOOD FORM
(By the Expert Wrinkler)

Is it good form to golf? That is a question I have been so repeatedly asked of late by correspondents that I can no longer postpone my answer. Now to begin with, I fear there is no doubt that golf is a little on the down grade—socially. Golf is no longer the monopoly of the best set, and I am told that artisans' clubs have actually been started in certain districts. The other day, as I was travelling in Lancashire, a man in the same compartment—with the most shockingly ill-cut trousers I ever saw—said to a friend, "I like 'Oylake, it's 'ealthy, and it's 'andy and within 'ail of 'ome." And it turned out that the chief attraction to him at Hoylake was the golf. Such an incident as this speaks volumes. But I always try to see both sides of every question, and there is unquestionably a great deal to be said in favour of golf. It was undoubtedly played by kings in the past, and at the present moment is patronised by grand dukes, dukes, peers and premiers.

BETWEEN FRIENDS.—*Mr. Spooner, Q.C. (a Neophyte).*
"This is my ball, I think?"   *Colonel Bunting (an
adept).* "By Jove, that's a jolly good 'lie'!"   *Mr.
Spooner.* "Really, Bunting, we're very old friends, of
course. But I do think you might find a pleasanter way
of pointing out a perfectly unintentional mistake!"

GOLF AND DRESS.

But the real and abiding attraction of golf is that it mercifully gives more opportunities to the dressy man than any other pastime. Football and cricket reduce everyone to a dead level in dress, but in golf there is any amount of scope for individuality in costume. Take the case of colour alone. The other day at Finsbury Park station I met a friend on his way home from a day's golfing, and I noticed that he was sporting the colours of no fewer than five different clubs. On his cap was the badge of the Camberwell Crusaders; his tie proved his membership of the Bickley Authentics; his blazer was that of the Tulse Hill Nondescripts; his brass waistcoat buttons bore the monogram of the Gipsy Hill Zingari; the roll of his knickerbocker stockings was embroidered with the crest of the Kilburn Incogs. The effect of the whole was, if I may be allowed the word, spicy in the extreme. Of course it is not everyone who can carry off such a combination, or who can afford to belong to so many first-class clubs. But my friend is a very handsome man, and has a handicap of *plus* two at Tooting Bec.

A Hero "Fin de Siècle."—*Podgers* (*of Sandboys Golf Club*). "My dear Miss Robinson, golf's the only game nowadays for the *men*. Lawn-tennis is all very well for you *girls*, you know."

KNICKERBOCKERS OR TROUSERS.

The burning question which divides golfers into two hostile camps is the choice between knickerbockers and trousers. Personally I favour the latter, but it is only right to explain that ever since I was gaffed in the leg by my friend Viscount —— when out cub-sticking with the Cottesmore I have never donned knickers again. To a man with a really well-turned calf and neat ankles I should say, wear knickerbockers whenever you get a chance. The late Lord Septimus Boulger, who had very thick legs, and calves that seemed to begin just above the ankles, used to wear knickerbockers because he said it put his opponent off his play. If I may say so without offence, he was a real funny chap, though a careless dresser, and I am told that his father, old Lord Spalding, has never been the same man since his death.

STOCKINGS AND CALVES.

Another advantage of knickerbockers is the scope they afford for the display of stylish stockings. A very good effect is produced by having a little red tuft, which should appear under

If you should find a stray bull in possession of the links, and who is fascinated by your little red landmarks, don't try and persuade poor Mr. Littleman to drive him away. He is very plucky—but it isn't golf.

the roll which surmounts the calf. The roll itself, which should always have a smart pattern, is very useful in conveying the impression that the calf is more fully developed than it really is. I noticed the other day at Hanger Hill that Sir Arlington Ball was playing in a pair of very full knickers, almost of the Dutch cut, and that his stockings— of a plain brown colour—had no roll such as I have described. Then of course Sir Arlington has an exceptionally well-modelled calf, and when in addition a man has £30,000 a year he may be allowed a certain latitude in his dress and his conduct generally.

BOOTS AND SHOES.

The question of footwear at golf is one of considerable difficulty, but there is a general feeling in favour of shoes. My friend the Tooting Bec *plusser* affects a very showy sort of shoe with a wide welt and a sort of fringe of narrow strips of porpoise hide, which fall over the instep in a miniature cataract. As regards the rival merits of india rubber studs on the soles and of nails, I compromise by a judicious mixture of

His First Round.—*Caddie* (*pointing to direction flag*). "You'd better play right on the flag, sir."
Curate. "Thank you very much. But I have very grave doubts as to my ability to hit such a very small mark at this distance!"

both. If a waistcoat be worn it should be of the brightest possible colour. I saw Lord Dunching the other day at Wimbledon Park in a charming waistcoat. The groundwork was a rich spinach green with discs of Pompeian red, and the buttons were of brass with his monogram in blue and white enamel in the centre. As it was a cold day he wore a mustard-coloured Harris tweed Norfolk jacket and a sealskin cap. Quite a large crowd followed him, and I heard afterwards that he had raised the record for the links to 193.

QUALIFICATIONS FOR A VALET.

One thing is certain—and that is we cannot all be first-class players. Personally, owing to the accident I have already referred to, I hardly ever play at all, but I always make it a point, if I am going on a visit to any place in the country where I know there are no golf links, to take a few nib-licks with me. A bag for clubs only costs a few shillings, and it looks well amongst your other paraphernalia on a journey. In engaging a valet again, always remember to ascertain whether he knows the rules of the " royal and ancient game."

EAR BLINKERS.—A suggestion for caddies of tender age in attendance on hot-tempered Anglo-Indian military gentlemen learning golf.

I shall never forget my humiliation when down at Lord Springvale's. As I was taking part in a foursome with the Hon. Agrippa Bramble, Lady Horace Hilton, and the second Mrs. Bunkeray, I got stuck in a furze-bush and my man handed me a putter. I could have cried with vexation.

ANSWERS TO CORRESPONDENTS.

CAVENDISH, CHATSWORTH.—As to the treatment of divots, different methods are recommended by different authorities. My plan, and I am not aware of a better, is to put them in my pocket when the caddie is not looking. When thoroughly dried they form an excellent peat for burning, or can be used for bedding out rhododendrons.

"NIL DESPERANDUM," BECKENHAM.—The best stimulant during match play is a beaten-up egg in a claret glass of sloe gin. The eggs are best carried in the pocket of your club-bag.

A. FLUBB, WOKING.—No, it is not good form to pay your caddie in stamps.

ALCIBIADES, WEMBLEY PARK.—If you must play golf on Sunday, I call it nothing short of hypocritical to go down to the links in a tall hat.

EVERY MAN TO HIS TRADE.—*Exasperated Amateur* (*to fore-caddie, who will* NOT *go on ahead*). "Go along, man. *Do* get on towards the next green." *Caddie.* "Beg pardin, Capting. You won't never get him to go no more than twenty yards ahead. 'E's been used to carrying a flag in front of a steam-roller."

133

LAYS FROM THE LINKS

I.—THE HISTORY OF A MATCH.

LET A be the Links where I went down to stay,
And B the man whom I challenged to play :—

    *   *   *   *   *

C was the Caddie no golfer's without,
D was the Driver I used going "out" :
E was the Extra loud " Fore !" we both holloa-ed,
F was the Foozle which commonly followed :
G was the Green which I longed to approach,
H was the Hazard which upset the coach :
I was B's Iron-shot (he's good for a younker),
J was his Joy when I pitched in the bunker.
K was the Kodak, that mischief-contriver,
L was B's Likeness—on smashing his driver :
M was the Moment he found out 'twas taken.
N was his Niblick around my head shaken :
O was the Oil poured on waters so stormy,
P was the Putt which, next hole, made me dormy.
Q was the Quality—crowds came to look on :
R the Result they were making their book on :
S was the Stymie I managed to lay,
T was Two more, which it forced him to play ;
U was the Usual bad work he let fly,
V was the Vengeance he took in the bye.

    *   *   *   *   *

W the Whisky that night : I must own
X was its quantity—wholly unknown ;
Y were the Yarns which hot whisky combine with,
Z was the Zest which we sang "*Auld Lang Syne*"

Short-sighted Lady Golfer. "Hi! have you seen a golf-ball fall anywhere here, please?"

[*Victim regards ball with remaining eye.*

II.—A TOAST.

FILL up your glasses !   Bumpers round
   Of Scotland's mountain dew !
With triple clink my toast you'll drink,
   The Links I pledge with you :
The Links that bind a million hearts,
   There's magic in their name,
The Links that lie 'neath every sky,
   And the Royal and Ancient Game !

A health to all who " miss the globe,"
   The special " stars " who don't ;
May thousands thrive to tee and drive
   As Jehu's self was wont !
No tee without a caddie—then
   The caddies will acclaim !
A health, I say, to all who play
   The Royal and Ancient Game !

Long life to all who face the foe,
   And on the green " lie dead " !—
An envied lot, as all men wot,
   For gallant "lads in red " :
Where balls fly fast and iron-shots plough
   Win medals, trophies, fame ;
Your watchword " Fore ! "   One cheer—two more—
   For the Royal and Ancient Game !

Then " *toe* and *heel* it " on the green
   (You'll make your partner swear),
But I'll be bound your dance, a round,
   With luck will end all square

Very mild Gentleman (who has failed to hit the ball five times in succession). "Well——"

Up-to-date Caddy (producing gramophone charged with appropriate expletives). "Allow me, sir!"

[*Mild Gentleman* DOES *allow him, and moreover presents him with a shilling for handling the subject in such a masterly manner.*

Win, lose, or halve the match—what odds?
  We love our round the same;
Though luck take wing, "the play's the thing,"
  The Royal and Ancient Game!

*   *   *   *   *

Then, Royal and Ancient Game, accept
  This tribute lay from me;
From me then take, for old sake's sake,
  This toast—Long life to thee!
A long, long life to thee, old friend—
  None worthier the name—
With three times three, long life to thee,
  O Royal and Ancient Game!

First Golfer (to *Second Golfer, who is caught in a bunker*). "Well, Jones told me this morning he did this hole yesterday in four." *Second Golfer* (*who stammers*). "If Jones s-s-said he did it in four, he was a 1-l-l———" *First Golfer*. "Steady, friend, steady!" *Second Golfer*. "——he was a l-lucky beggar!"

GOLF-LAND—HOLE BY HOLE

Match for a suit of oil-skins between Sunny Jack and Dismal Jimmy.

"The rain has beaten all records."—*Daily Papers.*
"Play the game."—*Modern motto.*

Hole 1.—Halved in 28. D. J. gets into the current with his 16th (a beauty) and is rescued by life-boat.

Hole 2.—Abandoned. A green-finder with a divining-rod, which is convertible into an umbrella, states that Primitive Baptists are using the green for purposes of total immersion.

Hole 3.—Abandoned. A regatta is found to be taking place in the big bunker.

Hole 4.—Halved in 23. S. J. discovered with life-belt round him which he has stolen from the flag. Reported death of a green-keeper, lost in trying to rescue two caddies from the bunker going to the 11th hole.

Hole 5.—Abandoned out of sympathy with the green-keeper.

Hole 6.—Abandoned. S. J. gets his driver

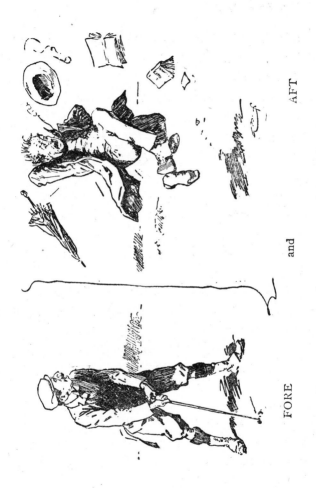

FORE and AFT

mixed in his life-belt, with the result that his braces burst. D. J. claims hole on the ground that no player may look for a button for more than two minutes. Mr. Vardon, umpiring from balloon, disallows claim. Both players take to canoes.

Hole 7.—D. J.'s canoe upset by body of drowned sheep as he is holing short put. Mr. Vardon decides that corpses are rubs on the green.

Hole 8.—Abandoned, owing to a fight for life-belt.

Hole 9.—Halved in 303, Mr. Vardon keeping the score.

Hole 10.—D. J. saves S. J.'s life. Hole awarded to S. J. by Mr. Vardon out of sympathy. S. J. one up.

Hole 11.—S. J. saves D. J.'s life and receives the Humane Society's monthly medal and the hole from Mr. Vardon as a reward of courage. S. J. two up.

Hole 12.—Abandoned. Collection made for the widows of drowned golfers, which realises ninepence. S. J. subsequently returns from a long, low dive.

Short-sighted Golfer (having been signalled to come on by lady who has lost her ball). "Thanks very much. And would you mind driving that sheep away?"

Holes 13 *and* 14.—Won by D. J. in the absence of S. J., who attends funeral water-games in honour of the green-keeper. All square.

Holes 15 *and* 16.—Abandoned by mutual consent, whisky being given away by the Society of Free-drinkers. Instant reappearance of the green-keeper.

Holes 17 *and* 18.—Unrecorded. Mr. Vardon declares the match halved.

Extract from the rules of a local golf club :— " RULE V.—The committee shall have the power at any time to fill any vacancy in their body."

A LESSON IN GOLF

"You won't dare!" said I.

"There is nothing else for it," said Amanda sternly. "You know perfectly well that we must practise every minute of the time, if we expect to have the least chance of winning. If she *will* come just now—well!" Amanda cocked her pretty chin in the air, and looked defiant.

"But—*Aunt Susannah*!" said I.

"It's quite time for you to go and meet her," said Amanda, cutting short my remonstrances; and she rose with an air of finality.

My wife, within her limitations, is a very clever woman. She is prompt: she is resolute: she has the utmost confidence in her own generalship. Yet, looking at Aunt Susannah, as she sat—gaunt, upright, and formidable—beside me in the dog-cart, I did not believe even Amanda capable of the stupendous task which she had undertaken. She would never dare——

I misjudged her. Aunt Susannah had barely

146

THE RETORT COURTEOUS.—*The Major-General waiting to drive, to girl carrying baby, who blocks the way*). "Now then, hurry on please with that baby." *Girl.* "Garn! Baby yerself, playing at ball there in your knickerbockers an' all!"

sat down—was, in fact, only just embarking on her first scone—when Amanda rushed incontinently in where I, for one, should have feared to tread.

" Dear Aunt Susannah," she said, beaming hospitably, " I'm sure you will never guess how we mean to amuse you while you are here ! "

" Nothing very formidable, I hope ? " said Aunt Susannah grimly.

" You'll never, never guess ! " said Amanda ; and her manner was so unnaturally sprightly that I knew she was inwardly quaking. " We want to teach you—what do you think ? "

" I think that I'm a trifle old to learn anything new, my dear," said Aunt Susannah.

I should have been stricken dumb by such a snub. Not so, however, my courageous wife.

" Well—golf ! " she cried, with overdone cheerfulness.

Aunt Susannah started. Recovering herself, she eyed us with a stony glare which froze me where I sat.

" There is really nothing else to do in these wilds, you know," Amanda pursued gallantly, though even she was beginning to look frightened.

A GOLF TOURNAMENT IN YE TIME OF YE ROMANS

From a rare old frieze (not) in ye British Museum.

149

"And it is such a lovely game. You'll like it immensely."

"*What* do you say it is called?" asked Aunt Susannah in awful tones.

"Golf," Amanda repeated meeekly; and for the the first time her voice shook.

"Spell it!" commanded Aunt Susannah.

Amanda obeyed, with increasing meekness.

"Why do you call it 'goff' if there's an 'l' in it?" asked Aunt Susannah.

"I—I'm afraid I don't know," said Amanda faintly.

Aunt Susannah sniffed disparagingly. She condescended, however, to inquire into the nature of the game, and Amanda gave an elaborate explanation in faltering accents. She glanced imploringly at me; but I would not meet her eye.

"Then you just try to get a little ball into a little hole?" inquired my relative.

"And in the fewest possible strokes," Amanda reminded her, gasping.

"And—is that all?" asked Aunt Susannah.

"Y—yes," said Amanda.

"Oh!" said Aunt Susannah.

" Anyway, it's better to break one's —— clubs than to lose one's —— temper ! ! "

A game described in cold blood sounds singularly insignificant. We both fell into sudden silence and depression.

"Well, it doesn't sound *difficult*," said Aunt Susannah. "Oh, yes, I'll come and play at ball with you if you like, my dears."

"*Dear* Auntie!" said Amanda affectionately. She did not seem so much overjoyed at her success, however, as might have been expected. As for me, I saw a whole sea of breakers ahead; but then I had seen them all the time.

We drove out to the Links next day. We were both very silent. Aunt Susannah, however, was in good spirits, and deeply interested in our clubs.

"What in the world do you want so many sticks for, child?" she inquired of Amanda.

"Oh, they are for—for different sorts of ground," Amanda explained feebly; and she cast an agonised glance at our driver, who had obviously overheard, and was chuckling in an offensive manner.

We both looked hastily and furtively round us when we arrived. We were early, however, and fortune was kind to us; there was no one else there.

"Perhaps you would like to watch us a little

A PLACE FOR EVERYTHING.—*Obstructive Lady (in reply to the golfer's warning call).* "The whole world wasn't made for golf, sir." *Youngster.* "No; but the links *wis*. 'Fore!'"

first, just to see how the game goes?" Amanda suggested sweetly.

"Not at all!" was Aunt Susannah's brisk rejoinder. I've come here to play, not to look on. Which stick——?"

"*Club*—they are called clubs," said Amanda.

"Why?" inquired Aunt Susannah.

"I—I don't know," faltered Amanda. "Do you Laurence?"

I did not know, and said so.

"Then I shall certainly call them sticks," said Aunt Susannah decisively. "They are not in the least like clubs."

"Shall I drive off?" I inquired desperately of Amanda.

"Drive off? Where to? Why are you going away?" asked Aunt Susannah. "Besides, you can't go—the carriage is out of sight."

"The way you begin is called driving off," I explained laboriously. "Like this." I drove nervously, because I felt her eye upon me. The ball went some dozen yards.

"That seems easy enough," said Aunt Susannah. "Give me a stick, child."

154

Unenviable position of Mr. Pottles, whose record drive has just landed fairly in the ribs of irascible old Colonel Curry, out for his constitutional canter.

" Not that end—the *other* end ! " cried Amanda, as our relative prepared to make her stroke with the butt-end.

" Dear me ! Isn't that the handle ? " she remarked cheerfully; and she reversed her club, swung it, and chopped a large piece out of the links. " Where is it gone ? Where is it gone ? " she exclaimed, looking wildly round.

" It—it isn't gone," said Amanda nervously, and pointed to the ball still lying at her feet.

" What an extraordinary thing ! " cried Aunt Susannah ; and she made another attempt, with a precisely similar result. " Give me another stick ! " she demanded. " Here, let me choose for myself—this one doesn't suit me. " I'll have that flat thing."

" But that's a putter," Amanda explained agonisedly.

" What's a putter ? You said just now that they were all clubs," said Aunt Susannah, pausing.

" They are all clubs," I explained patiently " But each has a different name."

" You don't mean to say you give them names like a little girl with her dolls ? " cried Aunt

Aunt Jabisca (pointing to earnest golfer endeavouring to play out of quarry). "Dear me, Maud, what a respectably dressed man that is breaking stones!"

Susannah. "Why, what a babyish game it is!" She laughed very heartily. "At any rate," she continued, with that determination which some of her friends call by another name, "I am sure that this will be easier to play with!" She grasped the putter, and in some miraculous way drove the ball to a considerable distance.

"Oh, splendid!" cried Amanda. Her troubled

brow cleared a little, and she followed suit, with mediocre success. Aunt Susannah pointed out that her ball had gone farther than either of ours, and grasped her putter tenaciously.

"It's a better game than I expected from your description," she conceded. "Oh, I daresay I shall get to like it. I must come and practise every day." We glanced at each other in a silent horror of despair, and Aunt Susannah after a few quite decent strokes, triumphantly holed out. "What next?" said she.

I hastily arranged her ball on the second tee: but the luck of golf is proverbially capricious. She swung her club, and hit nothing. She swung it again, and hit the ground.

"*Why* can't I do it?" she demanded, turning fiercely upon me.

"You keep losing you're feet," I explained deferentially.

"Spare me your detestable slang terms, Laurence, at least!" she cried, turning on me again like a whirlwind. "If you think I have lost my temper—which is absurd!—you might have the courage to say so in plain English!"

158

Suggestion for a rainy day.   Spillikins on a grand scale.

"Oh, no, Aunt Susannah!" I said. "You don't understand——"

"Or want to," she snapped. "Ot all silly games——"

"I mean you misunderstood me," I pursued, trembling. Your foot slipped, and that spoilt your stroke. You should have nails in your boots, as we have."

"Oh!" said Aunt Susannah, only half pacified. But she succeeded in dislodging her ball at last, and driving it into a bunker. At the same moment, Amanda suddenly clutched me by the arm. "Oh, Laurence!" she said in a blood-curdling whisper. "*What* shall we do? Here is Colonel Bartlemy!"

The worst had happened. The hottest-tempered man in the club, the oldest member, the best player, the greatest stickler for etiquette, was hard upon our track; and Aunt Susannah, with a red and determined countenance, was urging her ball up tne bunker, and watching it roll back again.

"Dear Auntie," said Amanda, in her sweetest voice, "you had much better take it out."

GOLF À **LA** WATTEAU—AND OTHERWISE

161

"Is that allowed?" inquired our relative suspiciously.

"Oh, you may always do that and lose a stroke!" I assured her eagerly.

"I shan't dream of losing a stroke!" said Aunt Susannah, with decision. "I'll get it out of this ditch by fair means, if I have to spend all day over it!"

"Then do you mind waiting one moment?" I said, with the calmness of despair. "There is a player behind us——"

"Let him stay behind us! I was here first," said Aunt Susannah; and she returned to her bunker.

The Links rose up in a hillock immediately behind us, so that our successor could not see us until he had reached the first hole. I stood with my eye glued to the spot where he might be expected to appear. I saw, as in a nightmare, the scathing remarks that would find their way into the Suggestion Book. I longed for a sudden and easy death.

At the moment when Colonel Bartlemy's rubicund face appeared over the horizon, Aunt

Major Brummel (comparing the length of his and his opponent's "drives"). "I think I'm shorter than Mr. Simkins?" *Small Caddie (a new hand, greatly flattered at being asked, as he thinks, to judge of their personal appearance).* "Yes, sir, and fatter too, sir!"

[*Delight of the gallant Major.*

Susannah, flushed but unconquered, drew herself up for a moment's rest from toil. He had seen her. Amanda shut her eyes. For myself, I would have run away shamelessly, if there had been any place to run to. The Colonel and Aunt Susannah looked hard at each other. Then he began to hurry down the slope, while she started briskly up it.

"Miss Cadwalader!" said the Colonel.

"Colonel Bartlemy!" cried Aunt Susannah; and they met with effusion.

I saw Amanda's eyes open, and grow round with amazed interest. I knew perfectly well that she had scented a bygone love affair, and was already planning the most suitable wedding-garb for Aunt Susannah. A frantic hope came to me that in that case the Colonel's affection might prove stronger than his zeal for golf. They were strolling down to us in a leisurely manner, and the subject of their conversation broke upon my astonished ears.

"I'm afraid you don't think much of these Links, after yours," Colonel Bartlemy was saying anxiously. "They are rather new——"

ARRY AT GOLF.

"Oh, I've played on many worse," said Aunt Susannah, looking round her with a critical eye. "Let me see—I haven't seen you since your victory at Craigmory. Congratulations!"

"Approbation from Sir Hubert Stanley!" purred the Colonel, evidently much gratified. "You will be here for the twenty-seventh, I hope?"

"Exactly what I came for," said Aunt Susannah calmly.

"Though I don't know what our ladies will say to playing against the Cranford Champion!" chuckled the Colonel; and then they condescended to become aware of our existence. We had never known before how exceedingly small it is possible to feel.

"Aunt Susannah, what am I to say? What fools you must think us!" I murmured miserably to her, when the Colonel was out of earshot looking for his ball. "We are such raw players ourselves —and of course we never dreamt——"

Aunt Susannah twinkled at me in a friendly manner. "There's an ancient proverb about eggs and grandmothers," she remarked cheerfully.

Miss Dora (to Major Putter, who is playing an important match, and has just lost his ball). "Oh, Major, do come and take your horrid ball away from my little dog. He won't let me touch it, and I know he must be ruining his teeth!"

"There should be a modern form for golf-balls
and aunts—hey, Laurence ? "

Amanda did not win the prize brooch ; but
Aunt Susannah did, in spite of an overwhelming
handicap, and gave it to her. She does not often
wear it—possibly because rubies are not becoming
to her : possibly because its associations are too
painful.

THE LOST GOLFER

[The sharp decline of ping-pong, whose attractions at its
zenith seduced many golfers from the nobler sport, has left
a marked void in the breasts of these renegades. Some of
them from a natural sense of shame hesitate to return to
their first love. The conclusion of the following lines
should be an encouragement to this class of prodigal.]

Just for a celluloid pillule he left us,
    Just for an imbecile batlet and ball,
These were the toys by which Fortune bereft us
    Of Jennings, our captain, the pride of us all.
Shopmen with clubs to sell handed him rackets,
    Rackets of sand-paper, rubber and felt,
Said to secure an unplayable service,
    Pestilent screws and the death-dealing welt.

Tennis Player (from London). "Don't see the fun o' this game—knockin' a ball into a bush, and then 'untin' about for it!"

THE AMERICAN HUSBAND

THE ENGLISH WIFE

Oft had we played with him, partnered him, sworn by
     him,
  Copied his pitches in height and in cut,
Hung on his words as he delved in a bunker,
  Made him our pattern to drive and to putt.
Benedick's with us, the major is of us,
  Swiper the county bat's still going strong;
He alone broke from the links and the clubhouse,
  He alone sank in the slough of ping-pong.

We have " come on "—but not his the example;
  Sloe-gin has quickened us—not his the cash;
Holes done in 6 where a 4 would be ample
  Vexed him not, busy perfecting a smash.
Rased was his name as a decadent angel,
  One more mind unhinged by a piffulent game,
One more parlour-hero, the worshipped of school-girls
  Who once had a princely " plus 5 " to his name.
Jennings is gone ; yet perhaps he'll come back to us,
  Healed of his hideous lesion of brain,
Back to the links in the daytime ; at twilight
  Back to his cosy club corner again.
Back for the medal day, back for our foursomes,
  Back from the tables' diminishing throng,
Back from the infantile, ceaseless half-volley,
  Back from the lunatic lure of ping-pong.

A TOO-FEEBLE EXPLETIVE

MacSymon. "I saw you were carrying for the professor yesterday, Sandy. How does he play?"

Sandy. "Eh, yon man 'll never be a gowffer. Div ye ken what he says when he foozles a ba'?"

MacSymon. "No. What does he say?"

Sandy. "'*Tut-tut!*'"

THE LINKS

'Tis a brilliant autumn day,
And the breeze has blown away
All the clouds that lowered gray;
      So methinks,
As I've half an hour to spare,
I will go and take the air,
While the weather still is fair,
        On the Links.

I admire the splendid view,
The delicious azure hue
Of the ocean and—when, *whew !*
      With a crack,
Lo ! there drops a little ball
Which elects to break its fall
By alighting on the small
        Of my back.

In the distance someone cries
Some remark about my eyes,
None too pleasant, I surmise,
      From the tone;
So away my steps I turn
Till a figure I discern,
Who is mouching by the burn
        All alone.

a Wallis
Mills
N.B.

THE MISERIES OF A *VERY* AMATEUR GOLFER

He is very shy, and unfortunately has to drive off in front of the lady champion and a large gallery. He makes a tremendous effort. The ball travels at least five yards!

He has lost a new " Eclipse,"
And a little word that slips
From his sulky-looking lips
      Tells me true
That, besides the missing ball,
Which is gone beyond recall,
He has lost—what's worst of all—
      Temper, too.

I conclude it will be best
If I leave him unaddressed,
Such a melancholy quest
      To pursue;
And I pass to where I spy
Clouds of sand uprising high
Till they all but hide the sky
      From the view.

They proceed, I understand,
From a bunker full of sand,
Where a golfer, club in hand,
      Freely swears
As he hacks with all his might,
Till his countenance is quite
As vermilion as the bright
      Coat he wears.

I observe him for a while
With a highly-tickled smile,
For it is the queerest style
      Ever seen :

Golfer. "And what's your name?"
Caddie. "They ca' me 'breeks,' but ma maiden name is Christy."

He is very short and stout,
And he knocks the ball about,
But he never gets it out
      On the green.

Still I watch him chop and hack,
Till I hear a sudden crack,
And the club-head makes a track
      In the light—
There's a startled cry of " FORE ! "
As it flies, and all is o'er !—
I remember nothing more
      Till to-night,

When I find myself in bed
With a lump upon my head
Like a penny loaf of bread;
      And methinks,
For the future I'll take care
When I want a little air,
That I won't go anywhere
      Near the Links.

"Mummy, what's that man for?"

DISTINCTION WITHOUT DIFFERENCE.—*Sensitive Golfer (who has foozled).* "Did you laugh at me, boy?" *Caddie.* "No, sir; I wis laughin' at anither man." *Sensitive Golfer.* "And what's funny about him?" *Caddie.* "He plays gowf awfu' like you, sir!"

Jones cannot see his ball anywhere, although he is positive
it fell about there somewhere.

NEVER HAVE A CADDIE WITH
A SQUINT!

(A Lay of the Links)

THEY told me he was skilful, and assiduous, and true,
    They told me he had "carried" for the bravest and the
      best.
His hair was soldier-scarlet, and his eyes were saucer blue,
    And one seemed looking eastward, whilst the other
      fronted west.
His strabismus was a startler, and it shook my nerve at
    once;
    It affected me with dizziness, like gazing from a height.

I straddled like a duffer, and I wavered like a dunce,
 And my right hand felt a left one, and my left felt far
  from right.
As I watched him place my ball with his visual axes
 crossed,
 The very sunshine glimmered, with a queer confusing
  glint,
I felt like a sick lubber on Atlantic surges tossed—
   Oh ! never have a caddie with a squint !

I'm an " irritable duffer "—so my enemies declare,—
 That is I'm very sensitive, and play a modest game.
A very little puts me off my stroke, and, standing there,
 With his boot-heels at right angles, and his optics much
  the same,
He maddened me—no less, and I felt that all success
 Against bumptious young McBungo—was impossible
  that day.
I'd have parted with a fiver to have beaten him.   His dress
 Was so very very swagger, and
  his scarlet cap so gay.
He eyed my cross-eyed caddie
 with a supercilious smirk,
 I tried to set my features, and
  my nerves, like any flint ;
But my " knicker'd " knees were
 knocking as I wildly set to
 work.

   Oh ! *never* have a caddie
   with a squint !

I tried to look away from the
 spoiler of my play,

But for fiendish fascination he was like a squinting
   snake;
All the muffings man can muff I contrived to muff that
   day;
   My eyes were all askew and my nerves were all
   ashake.
I seemed to squint myself, and not only with my eyes,
   My knees, my hands, my elbows, with obliquity were
   rife.
McBungo's sleek sham sympathy and sinister surprise
   Made almost insupportable the burden of my life.
He *was* so beastly friendly, and he *was* so blazing fair,
   So fulsomely effusive with suggestion, tip, and hint!
And all the while that caddie stood serenely cock-eyed
   there.
         Oh! *never* have a caddie with a squint!

Miss Binks was looking on! On that maiden I was
   gone,
   Just as she was gone on golf, in perfervid Scottish
   style.
On my merits with McBungo I should just about have
   won,
   But my shots to-day were such as made even Effie
   smile;
Oh, the lumps of turf I lifted! Oh, the easy balls I
   missed!
   Oh, the bunkers I got bogged in! And at last a gentle
   scorn
Curled the lips I would have given my pet "Putter" to
   have kissed.
   Such a bungler as myself her loved links had never
   borne;

ANOTHER LENTEN SACRIFICE.—*Golf Caddie (to Curate).* "High tee, sir?" *Curate.*
"No; put it on the ground. I give up sand during Lent."

And all the while McBungo — the young crocodile !— bewailed
What he called my "beastly luck," though his joy was plain as print,
Whilst that squint grew worse and worse at each shot of mine which failed.

Oh ! never have a caddie with a squint !

In "playing through the green" with my "brassie" I was seen
At most dismal disadvantage on that miserable day ;
He pointed through the rushes with cock-eyed, sardonic spleen,—
I followed his squint guidance, and I struck a yard away ;
But, oh ! 'twas worst of all, when I tried to hole the ball.
Oh, the ogre ! *How* he squinted at that crisis of the game !
His hideous strabismus held me helpless, a blind thrall
Shattered my nerves completely, put my skill to open shame.
That squint would, I am sure, have upset the solar system —

Voice from the Hill. "Now then, you young coward, don't stand about all day. Why don't you *take it away* from the dog?"

Oho ! the impish impudence, the gruesome goggle-glint !
The low, malicious chuckle, as he softly muttered, " Missed
'im ! "
No, *never* have a caddie with a squint !

Yet all the same McBungo did *not* get that rich Miss Binks,
Who was so sweet in every way, especially on golf.
He fancied he had cut me out that day upon those links,
But although he won the game—at golf, his love-game
came not off.
He and that demon caddie tried between them very hard
To shame me in the eyes of that dear enthusiast,
But—well, my clubs she carries, whilst McBungo, evil-
starred,
Was caught by a Scotch vixen with an obvious optic cast !
That's Nemesis, I say ! And she will not let him play
At the game he so adores. True she's wealthy as the
Mint.
At golf, with Effie, I have passed many a happy day,
But—we never have a caddie with a squint !

A caddie who's a duffer, or a caddie who gets drunk ;
A caddie who regards all other caddies as his foes ;
A caddie who will snigger when you fumble, fail or funk ;
A caddie who will whistle, or seems ever on the doze ;
A caddie who's too tiny, or too big and broad of bulk ;
A caddie who gets playing with your clubs upon the sly ;
A caddie who will chatter, or a caddie who will sulk ;
All these are calculated a golf devotee to try ;
All these are most vexatious to a golfer of repute ;
And still more so to a novice. But just take a friendly
hint !
Take a caddie who's a duffer, or a drunkard, or a brute,
But never try a caddie with a squint ! ! !

Boy (to young lady, who has been unfortunate enough to upset Colonel Bunker). "You'd better ride on before 'e gets 'is breath, miss!" Young Lady. "Why?" Boy. "I've 'eard 'im play golf ! ! !"

A GROWL FROM GOLFLAND

Bores there are of various species, of the platform, of the
quill,
Bores obsessed by Christian Science or the Education
Bill,
But the most exasperating and intolerable bore
Is the man who talks of nothing but the latest "rubber
core."

Place him in the Great Sahara, plant him on an Arctic
floe,
Or a desert island, fifteen thousand miles from Westward
Ho !
Pick him up a twelvemonth later, and I'll wager that you
find
Rubber filling *versus* gutty still and solely on his mind.

O American invaders, I accept your beef, your boots,
Your historical romances, and your Californian fruits ;
But in tones of humble protest I am tempted to exclaim,
" Can't you draw the line at commerce, can't you spare one
British game ? "

I am but a simple duffer ; I am quite prepared to state
That my lowest round on record was a paltry 88 ;
That my partner in a foursome needs the patience of a
Job,
That in moments of excitement I am apt to miss the
globe.

With my brassy and my putter I am very far to seek,
Generally slice to cover with my iron and my cleek ;
But I boast a single virtue : I can honestly maintain
I've escaped the fatal fever known as Haskell on the brain.

A golf case was recently before the Court of Appeal. Why
not a Golf Court on the links?

GOLF VICTOR!

Sir Golf and Sir Tennis are fighting like mad—
  Now Sir Tennis is blown, and Sir Golf's right above him,
And his face has a look that is weary and sad,
  As he hastily turns to the ladies who love him,
But the racket falls from him, he totters, and swirls,
As he hears them cry, "Golf is the game for the girls!"

*　　　*　　　*　　　*　　　*

The girls crave for freedom, they cannot endure
  To be cramped up at tennis in courts that are poky

And they are all of them certainly, perfectly sure
   That they'll never again touch " that horrible croquet,"
Where it's quite on the cards that they may play with papa,
And where all that goes on is surveyed by mamma.

To golf on the downs for the whole of the day
   Is " so awfully jolly," they keep on asserting,
With a good-looking fellow to teach you the way,
   And to fill up the time with some innocent flirting,
And it may be the maiden is woo'd and is won,
Ere the whole of the round is completed and done.

Henceforward, then, golf is the game for the fair—
   At home, and abroad, or in pastures colonial,
And the shouts of the ladies will quite fill the air
   For the links that will turn into bonds matrimonial,
And for husbands our daughters in future will seek
With the powerful aid of the putter and cleek !